# Little Red Riding Hood
## and the Lonely
# WOLF

Story by Maria West    Pictures by Chris Lensch

For Giovi,
You will always have
a warm, cozy home
and a family who
loves you.
-M.W.

First published by Experience Early Learning Company
7243 Scotchwood Lane, Grawn, Michigan 49637 USA

ISBN: 978-1-937954-36-9
Visit us at www.ExperienceEarlyLearning.com

# Little Red Riding Hood
## and the Lonely
# WOLF

Story by Maria West    Pictures by Chris Lensch

Once upon a time, deep in the forest, there lived a lonely wolf. He spent his days dreaming of finding a family to love him.

Near Wolf's home was a tiny cottage where a kind grandmother lived. Each week, her granddaughter, Little Red Riding Hood, would come to visit and bring her treats of the yummiest sort.

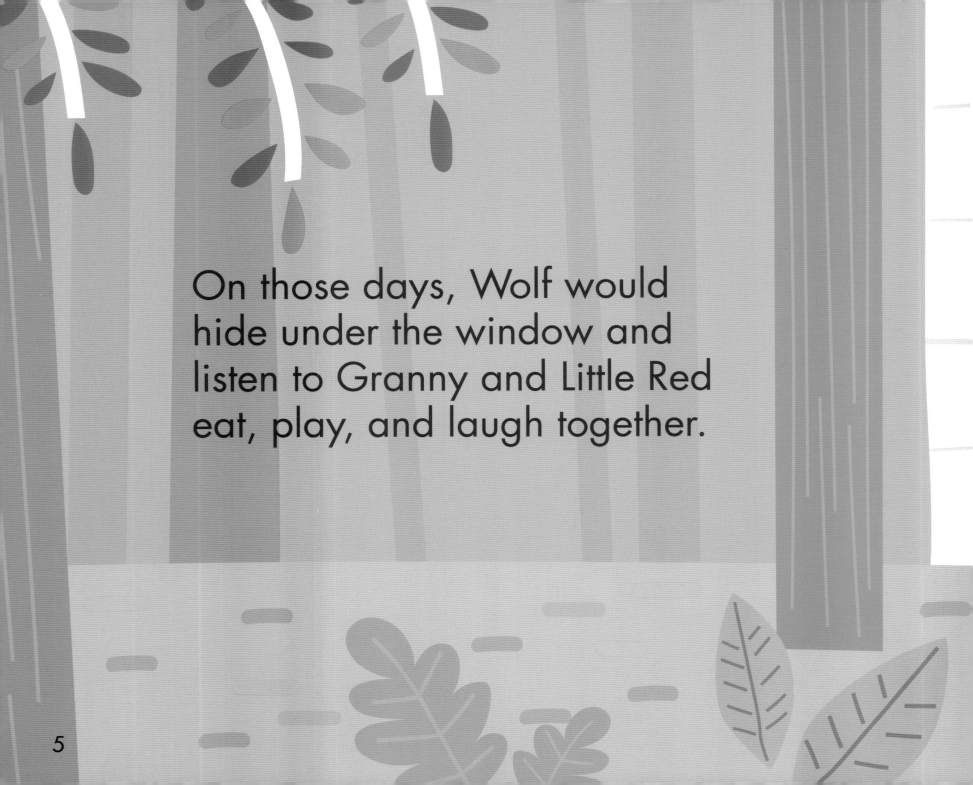

On those days, Wolf would hide under the window and listen to Granny and Little Red eat, play, and laugh together.

He would smell bread baking in the oven
and feel the warmth coming from the fire.
Wolf wanted very much to live with Granny,
but he stayed away.

9

You see, not too long ago, there was a situation with a very bad wolf and three little pigs. Now everyone was afraid of wolves.

One day, Granny left to go to the market. Wolf thought to himself, "Maybe I can just take a peek inside to see what it feels like in such a cozy home." And so he crept inside.

No sooner than Wolf had snuck in Granny's home when he heard, "Granny! I have come to bring you cakes and treats!" It was Little Red Riding Hood!

Wolf panicked! He quickly threw on Granny's robe, sleeping cap, and socks and jumped into her bed to hide.

Finding her Granny in bed, Little Red asked in a worried voice, "Granny, are you feeling okay today?" But the frightened wolf only replied with a whimper.

"Oh my, Granny," said Little Red. "You look terrible!" Wolf nodded his head carefully.

16

"What big eyes you have today, Granny!" said Little Red. "You must have a headache."

Wolf whimpered again, and so Little Red fluffed up the pillow to make him more comfortable.

"Granny," said Little Red, "what big feet you have sticking out from under your blanket! They must be very cold!"

Wolf whimpered once more, and so Little Red put a quilt over his feet.

"My, what a big nose you have, Granny!" said Little Red. "You need a tissue, you poor thing."

21

Wolf gave a sniffle, and Little Red brought him tissues then fed him warm soup and a muffin.

Then Little Red read him a story and sang him a song. Wolf had never felt so cared for.

"This must be what it is like to have a family," he thought to himself. He smiled and closed his eyes.

Just as Wolf was nodding off, the door opened and in walked Granny. Little Red Riding Hood looked at her, shocked and confused.

She dropped the tray she was carrying and cried out, "If you are Granny, who is that in your bed?"

The wolf hid under the covers and began to cry.

But Granny was old and wise. She knew that the Wolf meant them no harm. In fact, she even understood how he felt. She lived alone in the woods too and without Little Red's visits she would be very lonely.

"You can come out from under the covers, Wolf," said Granny gently. But the wolf was too afraid.

And so Granny hummed the wolf a song. As he listened, he thought back to all of the times he hid under the window and listened to Granny and Red sing songs. It made him feel warm inside.

He felt loved.

And so, he popped out of the covers, wagged his tail and licked Granny on the nose to say thank you.

They played together all afternoon. They laughed and ate Little Red's treats. When it was time for dinner, Granny invited Wolf to stay – forever!

Each week, Little Red Riding Hood came to visit Granny and Wolf.

They lived happily ever after-

as a family.

The End